Believe in your Dreams ;

Buddy's Magic Window

A Little Dog's BIG Adventure

Photography and story by Dennis Glennon

Acknowledgments

To my love Angela Criscuoli, who surprised me by sneaking my book files to Staples and printing out the first hardcover version of *Buddy's Magic Window,* prompting me to finally get this book out to the world.

To my mom and dad, Marianne and Eugene Glennon, who never stopped encouraging me to pursue my dreams. I love you. It has been some journey.

To Linda (Traci) Morigi who is a dear friend, and Buddy's breeder through her Blue Mountains Goldens kennel. Buddy was bred from her dog Angel. She, her husband Paul and son Stephen became great friends. Dogs bring good people together.

To Patty McCoy-Coleman, co-breeder of Buddy whose dad's name is Ch. McCoy N Adams Family Reunion Chandler. Chandler is co-owned by Robert Mahon. Patty is a great friend and wonderful soul and has been a tremendous help throughout my career.

To Donna Lynch, Buddy's Mom. We photographed many of the Buddy images on her property, including the famous cover shot. Donna's daughters, Michelle and Nicole, joined us on the photoshoot—a fun day we will never forget. Donna's family are some of the kindest and most generous people anyone could know.

To my family who supported and encouraged me through all my adventures—Kevin, Kelly & Jim, and Tim & Kathleen. I am so glad we can share this moment.

To Joanne and Stan Silver, dear friends who introduced me to the dog world.

I am also blessed to have the best friends in the world. My friends listed here had a very direct impact on my success with this book.

Pat & Tracy Moyna, Kevin & Karen Lee. Craig & Christina Tutschek, Glen and Mary Tutschek. Pat & May Cabral. Rich Walker. Rob Tormo, Doreen Towers Shammas. Mark Adessa. Sara Watters. Peter Huntoon. Michelle Nicodemo. Nina Stanson. Julie Korogodon. Jeff & Betsy Ball. Jody Whitsell. Michaela Brody Zalco. Jody Weinberg and her family. Thank you for all the love and support.

To some of my photo buddies—James and Karen Ronan, Andrew Thompson, and Terry Chick—all of whom have shared in, and are responsible for, much of my success.

To Jay and Marvin Miletsky. I met Marvin while getting a copy of my book at Staples. He introduced me to Jay who is now guiding me and facilitating getting *Buddy's Magic Window* printed.

To Karen and Hugh McDiarmid. Karen is my graphic designer who took what was in my mind and laid it out perfectly bringing my book to life. Her professional talent is unreal, but her kindness and patience are a Godsend. Hugh was my editor and massaged my "novel" back to a kid's book length. LOL. Yes, I write like I talk.

To Carl R. Sams and Jean Stoick. Carl and Jean have been mentors to me and more helpful then they may ever know. I would not be where I am without their guidance.

To my Kickstarter Backers. You are the "Puppy Breath" that brought *Buddy's Magic Window* to life. We are forever connected through this wonderful book.

To Rachel and Ichabod. My first dog models.

And a big shout out to BUDDY—the star of the show!

Copyright 2020 Dennis Glennon

All Rights Reserved. No part of this book may be reproduced in any manner without the author's written consent except in the case of brief excerpts in critical reviews and articles.

Inquiries about this book or photographic prints should be addressed to the publisher:

Dennis Glennon Photography
201-343-8889
DennisGlennon.com

Art Director/Graphic Design: Karen McDiarmid Design, LLC
Color Expertise: Greg Dunn of Digital Imagery, LLC
Editor: Hugh McDiarmid

Printed and bound July 2020
Printed in China

Glennon, Dennis
Buddy's Magic Window
Written and photographed by Dennis Glennon

SUMMARY: A puppy's tale of his adventure through the woods, learning valuable life lessons: trusting his heart, having great faith, and believing anything is possible.

ISBN: 978-0-692-40873-5
Library of Congress Control Number: 2020906288

10 9 8 7 6 5 4 3 2

For those who rescue animals.

Buddy was resting on the porch
one spring morning when the
sky turned dark.

He looked for his mom and dad.
He looked for
his brothers and sisters,
but Buddy was
all alone.

Buddy was scared!

Suddenly...

thunder BOOMED!

and lightning FLASHED!

Now Buddy was VERY scared!

He scrambled off the porch
and he ran!

He ran away from the
scary thunder,
away from the bright lightning,
away from the dark, dark sky.

He raced
into the foggy forest.

Buddy ran fast and far.

And soon he was

very,

very

lost.

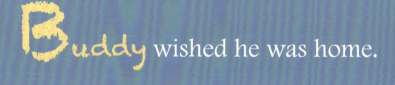Buddy wished he was home.

He didn't like being lost.

He didn't like being alone.

The rain stopped.
Buddy knew it was time to
find his way home.

"Maybe if I can get higher
I will see my way home,"
he thought.

He climbed **WAY** up
to the top of a rocky ledge.

But he did not see
his house.

The climbing made him
very tired.

He plopped down on a wooden bridge
that crossed a small woodland stream
and wondered,

"Will I EVER get home?"

Buddy peered down at the gurgling stream.

Then he noticed a forest path in the distance.

"Maybe that's the way home!"

Near the path was a
beautiful butterfly.

"I'm trying to find my home," he told her.

The butterfly waved her wings and kindly replied,
"I wish I could help, but I am just a simple butterfly.
There are stronger and wiser creatures at the pond.
Follow the path."

When Buddy reached the pond
he saw a colorful turtle sunning himself
and barked,
"Can you help me find my home?!"

The frightened turtle cried, "Don't eat me!"

"I won't eat you," said Buddy,
but the turtle had already disappeared
under the water.

Buddy said hello to a frog . . .

. . . but the frog just eyed him suspiciously.

Buddy saw a friendly looking moose across the pond.

He crawled into a canoe at the water's edge and shouted, "Can you help me find my way home?"

The moose smiled.
"I know every inch of this forest. I can help you."

Buddy told the moose
he didn't live in the forest.

"Oh my!" exclaimed the moose.
"Then you need a wiser and more well-traveled creature than I.
Follow the path at the end of the pond.
Good luck!"

Buddy thanked the moose
as he watched some loons float by
with their newborn.

He gave a short bark and they quickly swam away.
Buddy thought,
"They must be loony!"

He watched another duck run across the pond.
"Oh no, a retriever!" she squawked.

"I wont hurt you!"
Buddy yelled,
but the duck was gone.

Buddy followed the moose's advice and
off he went to find the path out of the forest.
Along the way he met
a mother moose with two young calves.

"How much farther to the end of the pond?"
he asked her.

"Not far," she answered,
but go right when the path splits.
Danger lies to the left, friends to the right. Good luck."

When Buddy came to the split in the path
he remembered the mother moose's warning,
"Danger to the left, friends to the right!"

But Buddy was very young.
He didn't know which way was left or right.

So, he chose a path.

Very soon he **KNEW** it was
the **WRONG** path!

His mommy had told him about foxes,
"They are quite sneaky and like to play tricks."

Buddy turned around and he *RAN!*

He ran back to the split in the trail
and quickly followed the right path out of the forest.

Buddy was led into a clearing.

Moo, MOO, MOOO-VE!!

Buddy tilted his head and listened.

"What could that be?" he wondered.

Buddy ran into an old barn and jumped
high up onto the tractor seat
to try to see what could be making this silly noise.

A herd of cows were out in the pasture.
The cows stared at Buddy.

"Can you help me find my home?"
Buddy called. But the cows just stared.

One nutty brown cow made a rude face at Buddy.

He decided they were not very helpful.

Buddy continued along the path.
A chubby faced chipmunk was storing nuts in his cheeks,
getting ready for winter.

Buddy asked, "Can you help me find my way home?"

The well-mannered chipmunk didn't answer right away.
He knew not to talk with his mouth full.

"No, but I have some nuts I can share with you."

Buddy had forgotten how hungry he was.
The nuts were delicious.

Chirp, Chirp, Chirp . . .

Buddy heard a bluebird sing.

"Can you help me find my way home, Mr. Bluebird?"

"The wise owl will know," the bluebird answered.
"He is perched high in the Great Tree
overseeing the forest and beyond.
But hurry little puppy! It's getting late and
Mr. Great Horned Owl flies at night."

Buddy raced to find the wise owl.
"Who? Who? Who, are you?" screeched the great horned owl.

"I am Buddy. I am lost and can't find my way home.
Can you help me?"

The Great Horned Owl cocked his head and thought.

"There is a barn farther down the path.
Go inside, climb up the hay into the magic window.
Look through it. Listen to the whispers on the wind.
Trust in your heart. Believe in yourself.
If your faith is strong,
the magic window will take you home.

Buddy could see
the barn with the Magic Window.

He ran inside and climbed up the hay.
He found the Magic Window the wise owl had told him about!

It didn't look magic to Buddy, but from it,
he could see all the places he'd been:

The Deep Woods   The Rock Ledge   The Bridge

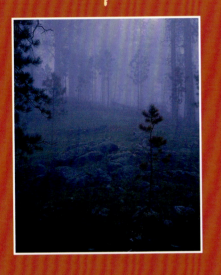
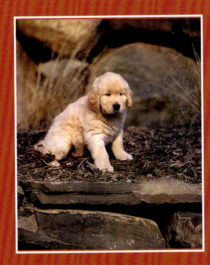
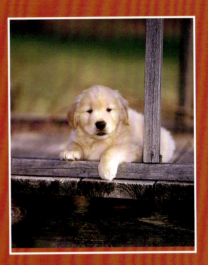

The Forest Path   The Pond

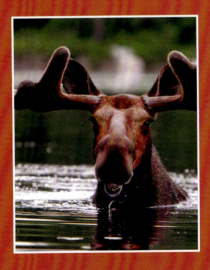

But he did not see his home.

Buddy remembered the words
of the wise owl.

He listened for the whispers on the wind.
Buddy trusted in his heart.
His faith was strong.

He could see his family
searching for him.
He felt how much they missed him.
He then pictured himself
at home with them.

Suddenly,
by the power of the
Magic Window
Buddy was lifted
home!

"I think I hear Buddy!
Is that him panting on the porch?"

Buddy seemed to appear from nowhere.

"Hey everyone!
I'm finally home!"

Buddy told his family about how
the loud thunder
and scary lightning made him run
into the woods.

He told them how he'd asked
the forest animals for help
and how the great horned owl had led him home.

After telling his family all about his adventures,
Buddy was very, **VERY** tired.
He drifted off to sleep
in his favorite place.

He knew he wanted to explore the world again one day.
He wanted to visit with the friendly animals
that had helped him along the way:

the moose,

the butterfly,

the chipmunk...

but **NOT** the **FOX!**

For now though,
Buddy was just glad to be home
with his family.

The big world and magic window adventures
were puppy-tales he'd save
for another day.